MW00327782

200 Tips
for Growing

FLOWERS

in the

PACIFIC NORTHWEST

200 Tips

for Growing

FLOWERS

in the

PACIFIC NORTHWEST

Barbara Ashmun

CHICAGO
REVIEW
PRESS

Library of Congress Cataloging-in-Publication
Data

Ashmun, Barbara
  200 tips for growing flowers in the Pacific
Northwest / by Barbara Ashmun. — 1st. ed.
      p.   cm.
  Includes index.
  ISBN 1-55652-253-3 (pbk.)
  1. Flower gardening—Northwest, Pacific.
  I. Title.
SB405.5.N67A88   1996
635.9′0979—dc20   95-37094
                                              CIP

Published by Chicago Review Press, Incorporated
814 North Franklin Street
Chicago, Illinois 60610

ISBN 1-55652-253-3

5 4 3 2 1

CONTENTS

ACKNOWLEDGMENTS

There is no way to accurately list all the gardening friends, teachers, students, and clients from whom I have gleaned these tips over the past twenty years— too many generous souls have shared their secret recipes for success for my overloaded memory.

I am, however, especially grateful to gardeners, nursery owners, and designers with experience in climates different from my own, who were so willing to share the problems and solutions particular to their area, especially the following:

Karen Brown, Brown's Nursery, Lincoln City, Oregon

John Clements, Heirloom Old Garden Roses, St. Paul, Oregon

Bobbi Feyerabend, Oakland, California

Beth Holland, Cannon Beach, Oregon

Nicola Luttropp, Lamb Nursery, Long Beach, Washington (formerly in Spokane, Washington)

Ruth Mackey, Portland, Oregon

Libby and George McGeary, Bend, Oregon

Parker Sanderson, Christmas Valley, Oregon

The Staff of Portland Nursery, Portland, Oregon

A special thanks to my book agent, Betsy Amster, whose impeccable standards have stimulated me to polish my writing. And my ongoing gratitude to my friends in the Monday Night Writing Group who encourage, support and revitalize me: Nancy Woods, Jebra Turner, Anita Witt, Cindy McKitrick, Trudy Hussman, Carol Woodford, Jonna Selene, and Jolinda Osborne.

INTRODUCTION

I'm crazy about flower gardening. I've spent most of the last twenty years growing every flowering plant I can get my hands on. When I'm not gardening I'm showing homeowners how to create colorful flower gardens in their own yards, visiting gardens all over the world, and teaching classes.

Gardeners are inquisitive, ingenious, and generous, so I learn as much as I teach. I can tell from my students' and clients' questions and comments how important it is to share the down-to-earth tips that experienced gardeners pass across the backyard fence. Often these methods gleaned from years of hands-on gardening get left out of books, so it is just this kind of information that I want to offer you. In particular, I'd like to pass on what I've learned about the best flowering plants for the Pacific Northwest, techniques for growing them well, and pointers for placing them together in the garden to create beautiful compositions.

Many flowering plants grow easily here, and the evidence lies in the popularity of gardening and the abundance of commercial growers. We in the Pacific Northwest are fortunate to have the tempering influence of the Pacific Ocean's Japan Current. Our winters are not too cold, with average lows in the twenties–more commonly we complain about the rain, which is plentiful in the winter and spring. Our summers are not too hot–a few rare days over ninety degrees and we begin to wilt, for mostly we are accustomed to weather in the seventies and eighties. Dryness can be a problem in the summer and fall, at least for our plants–we have little of the oppressive humidity of the east and south.

For the most part we must learn which plants adapt well to lots of moisture in the winter and spring followed by dryness in the summer and fall. Many of us begin with heavy clay soil, some with rocky or sandy soil, which we moan and groan about at first. Eventually those of us determined to garden learn to amend the soil and take pride in this horticultural alchemy.

We have our share of pests, predators, and weeds that like the good growing conditions as much as our cultivated plants. Slugs, aphids, moles, deer, and rabbits were here before us and will be here after we are gone, and we invent various ways of discouraging them from ravaging our gardens. Blackberry, morning glory, fireweed, thistle, dock, horsetail, and buttercup are just a few of the weeds that compete with our flowers, but we discover how to throttle them and protect our gardens from hostile takeovers.

The Pacific Northwest includes a fair number of gardening zones with differing weather patterns, soil composition, and populations of native plants. To round out my own hands-on experience I have consulted with nursery owners and gardeners in other parts of the Northwest—I am grateful to them for their generous contributions.

Like any other passion, gardening comes complete with problems to solve; once early difficulties are mastered, new ones continue to present themselves. These challenges give gardeners the chance to develop patience, determination, tolerance, imagination, and ingenuity. There is no end to the process, thank goodness. When you open the door to gardening you enter a boundless territory.

COPING WITH THE WEATHER

1 **Every climate in the Pacific Northwest has its advantages and disadvantages—gardeners take heart and count your blessings.** A wet climate nourishes the plants and cuts down on the job of watering. It also means that weeds will grow quickly and slugs will thrive, so time saved on watering will be spent yanking weeds and hunting slugs. Windy climates prevent build up of mildew and aphids but dry out the soil quickly, requiring heavy mulching and regular irrigation. Maritime gardens benefit from the tempering effect of the ocean, yet suffer from salty winds.

I

2 **Plant climate zones tell you the cumulative effects of weather through the seasons, and help you figure out which plants to grow.** Useful garden books tell you in which zones a plant will do well. Latitude, elevation, the ocean, mountains and hills, and the continental air mass all influence climate. There are about a dozen climate zones in the Pacific Northwest (Western and Eastern Washington, Western and Eastern Oregon, Idaho, Montana, and Northern California).

3 **Take good advantage of micro climates within your garden and think about creating them, too.** Beds along the south side of your house will naturally heat up sooner in the spring and stay warm longer into the fall, than the cooler, shadier beds on the north side. You can create a milder microclimate by building a low stone wall that will hold warmth, and grow heat-loving plants on its south side.

4 **Where the growing season is short due to frost and cool evenings, construct raised beds.** The soil in raised beds will warm up faster and dry out sooner than in conventional beds, making it easier to get your plants off and running in the spring. Of course they will also require more frequent watering in the summer and fall.

5 In areas of extremes, where summers are hot and dry, yet winters are cold, look to the toughest herbaceous perennials for color. Daylilies, most iris, peonies, hosta, most flowering onions (*Allium*), and oriental poppies are super-hardy plants with strong root systems and the ability to weather heat and cold.

6 In the coldest parts of the Pacific Northwest, try the extremely winter-hardy Rugosa roses and the Canadian Hardy roses (zones 3–9). Rugosa roses, especially the species, *Rosa rugosa*, *Rosa rugosa alba*, and *Rosa rugosa rubra*, make terrific shrubs for hedging, screening, or backdrop, with beautiful foliage, repeat blooming flowers, fragrance, and showy autumn fruit. Canadian Hardy roses are also repeat blooming shrubs: 'John Cabot' has deep rose-pink flowers; 'John Franklin' and 'Alexander MacKenzie' are red.

7 Where drought is a problem, whether due to low rainfall or wind, take advantage of fleshy-leaved plants that store water and gray-leaved plants that prefer dry conditions. Sedums, succulents, lavender, rosemary, sage, artemisia, thyme, yarrow, and dianthus thrive in a dry climate with plenty of summer heat.

3

8 **In harsher, mountainous zones of the Pacific Northwest, grow selected cultivars of native plants that are hardy in your area.** For example, *Penstemon davidsonii menziesii* and *Penstemon newberryi*, native to the high mountains of Sierra Nevada, are hardy in zones 1–7, just like *Penstemon rupicola*, native to the Cascade and Siskiyou mountains. All adapt well to high elevation areas with good soil drainage, and have cultivars with showier flowers than the wild forms, such as *Penstemon davidsonii menziesii* 'Broken Top', *Penstemon newberryi* 'Red Lassen Form', and *Penstemon rupicola* 'Diamond Lake'.

9 **In coastal areas of the Pacific Northwest, counter the effects of wind by constructing fences and hedges.** Fences, walls, and hedges can help a great deal to cut down the desiccation and breakage caused by wind. At the beach, shore pine (*Pinus contorta*) and *Escallonia* make good windbreaks. Small starter plants will have an easier time adjusting to coastal weather than big plants brought in from kinder climates.

10 **If you garden at the coast, take advantage of flowers that love the mild climate and can take the salty**

wind and sandy soil. Montbretia, thrift (*Armeria*), lavender, artemisia, santolina, rosemary, pincushion flower (*Scabiosa*), nasturtium, signet marigold (*Tagetes tenuifolia*), African daisy (*Osteospermum*), and portulaca thrive at the beach. Sweet peas and honeysuckle do well on fences. A little further inland from the strong winds, or in sheltered places, calla lilies, dahlias, fuchsias, geraniums (*Pelargonium*), and hydrangeas thrive in the damp coastal air.

11 **If you garden in Northern California where mild winters are an advantage but drought is a problem, borrow Mediterranean, Mexican, and Australian plants that like the heat and tolerate less water.** To add to the palette of native plants, choose perennials from other parts of the world with similar climates: penstemon, rosemary, santolina, germander, sunroses, Mexican evening primrose (*Oenothera berlandieri*), yarrow, hardy cranesbills (*Geranium*), 'Hopley's Purple' oregano, all the many cultivars of lavender and sage (*Salvia*).

12 **Even though Western Washington and Western Oregon have very rainy winters and springs, and summer days can be cool and**

overcast, actual rainfall in summer and fall is meager and you must water. Gray days and cool evenings can lull a gardener into complacency. Pay attention to the soil, and water when it feels dry to the touch. A long soak for half an hour or more once or twice a week will do your flowers more good than frequent scanty watering.

GOOD DIRT: BUILDING A STRONG FOUNDATION

❀ ❀ ❀

The best soil for growing flowers holds enough moisture to nourish the plants, yet is also crumbly enough to allow air to reach the roots and to let the excess water drain out. The most desirable dirt is a balanced mixture of clay, silt, and sand. Clay holds water, but too much of it keeps the soil wet, slippery, and cold. Sand promotes good drainage, allowing the soil to warm up quickly, but an excess amount lets the ground dry out too quickly.

14 If you want a scientific analysis of your soil, contact your county extension service for information about local testing sources. Some cities have soil tests available for a modest price through state agricultural programs. Where these are unavailable, commercial laboratories can help for a slightly higher fee. A thorough test will determine the amount of major nutrients in the soil (nitrogen, phosphorus, and potassium) as well as trace elements (calcium, magnesium, boron, zinc, iron, copper, manganese). It should also inform you about the pH of your soil—if it is acidic or alkaline. A good report describes your soil texture— the percentages of sand, silt, and clay—and recommends what to add to your soil.

15 Add plenty of organic matter to improve the texture of soil that has too much clay or too much sand. Compost—the broken-down material from kitchen waste, leaves, weeds, and grass clippings—is my favorite soil amendment. Well-rotted manure, peat moss, gypsum, rotted straw, and sawdust will all help.

16 Mixing in gypsum, pumice, per lite, and crushed rock will improve the drainage of heavy clay soil.

Just about any material that gets between the clay particles helps to make space for water and air to drain through.

◣17◥ Loosen the soil first by hand digging or tilling. Then add organic matter and fertilizer and work them in well. A loose soil will be much easier for you to plant in, weed, and dig in when it's time to lift your plants for division. Turn the soil over to at least a shovel's depth and break it up into small crumbs. Then spread compost and fertilizer over the top, turn it all again, and rake it smooth.

◣18◥ Fertilizer formulas tell you the percentage of nitrogen, phosphorus, and potassium, in that order. Whether it's a box of rose food or a sack of bonemeal, three numbers appear to tell you what's inside. 15–10–5, for example, means that the material is 15 percent nitrogen, 10 percent phosphorus, and 5 percent potassium. The other 70 percent is filler, so the higher the numbers on the container, the more fertilizer is really inside.

◣19◥ To promote healthy green leaves, add nitrogen to the soil. Bloodmeal, recycled sewage sludge, cottonseed meal, bat guano, poultry manure, and rabbit manure are rich in nitrogen. It's especially important to add nitrogen to the soil if you've mulched the ground with wood products (bark dust, sawdust), which consume nitrogen as they break down. Too much nitrogen may cause your plants to be bigger than is beneficial (plants that get huge are also likely to topple over in rain and wind).

20 **Add phosphorus to the soil to increase flower and fruit production.** Bonemeal and rock phosphate are the two highest sources of phosphorus for your garden. I routinely sprinkle bonemeal in the planting hole whenever I add new perennials to the border.

21 **Add potassium for early growth, stem strength, and plant vigor.** Wood ashes, seaweed, hay, guano, granite dust, and greensand are good sources of potassium. Granite dust and greensand, being mineral, are slower to break down than ashes, seaweed, hay, and guano, their plant and animal counterparts.

22 **Compost bins provide a tidy, space-saving place to make your own compost.** A series of three simple bins, each about 4 feet tall and

4 feet wide, can be built from wood, wood and metal mesh, cement block, or even recycled wooden pallets. Start by filling the first bin with weeds, leaves, and grass clippings. After a while turn the material into the second bin, let it rot there for a month or so, then turn it into the third bin where it will complete its breakdown. It's important to keep the debris damp. Some folks like to layer green matter and soil to speed the process. Throw in any extra earthworms lying around after a rainfall to help transform the raw material into compost.

⟨23⟩ If you're not in a big hurry, make your compost pile where you want next year's new bed, and just let it rot. Every summer I start a new bed by piling leaves and grass clippings about 5 feet high on top of the lawn. All this debris smothers the existing grass and breaks down to a raised bed about a foot and a half tall full of rich dirt by the next spring.

LAYING OUT YOUR GARDEN

24 **Start planning your garden with a rough sketch of the areas you want to develop.** A simple drawing of your house and garden, and a list of what you want to use your garden for, will help you map out the spaces within your property. Note which areas are sunny and which are shady, and where the doors and windows are located. Perhaps you'd like a cutting garden, or raised beds for vegetables—sketch these into a sunny place. You might like an outdoor dining area near the kitchen door. A work area with room for composting and potting up might fit toward the back of the property. A backyard lawn with room for the children to play might be useful where it's sunny and flat. Note possible places for these needs on your plan.

25 **For a more accurate plan, use graph paper and a scale.** To visualize exactly how much room you're working with, measure your home and property and draw it to scale on a piece of graph paper. An engineer's scale or even a ruler can be used to draw up a plan in which ¼ inch on paper represents 1 foot of garden space. Measure distances and draw in any existing trees or shrubs in relationship to each other and to the house and the property lines.

26 **Copy off several blank to-scale drawings so that you can play around with a few versions of your plan.** It's much easier to experiment on paper than in the ground. With several copies of the blank plan, you can try out any number of tentative designs. Experiment freely with the shapes of paths and beds, and with the placement of plants.

27 **If you prefer, you can make your drawing right on the ground.** I like to plan out in the garden where I can see the whole picture. I use flexible hoses to mark out the shapes of curved paths and beds. I stick stakes in the ground to represent trees and shrubs. Straight-edged beds and paths can be marked off with stakes and string. I leave these markings out for a while to study them from different points of view and readjust them as needed.

28 **Pay attention to creating pictures to look at from your windows.** Each window of your home is a potential frame for a garden scene. Every time you stand at the kitchen window you can enjoy the composition that is in its view.

29 **In the Pacific Northwest, where winters are overcast, include plenty of winter color to enjoy from frequently used windows.** I love looking out my kitchen window at dozens of white and pink lenten roses (*Helleborus orientalis*) and pink 'Dawn' viburnum (*Viburnum bodnantense* 'Dawn'), blooming together in February.

30 **Be sure to place fragrant plants outside the windows so you can get whiffs of their scent indoors.** The previous owner of my house planted a white lilac right outside the bedroom window—it sends its perfume into the house every spring. I added dwarf sweet box (*Sarcococca*) for winter and Hall's honeysuckle for summer near the front door.

31 **Since many flowering plants are billowy, remember to include a few architectural plants for focal points.** Perennials with definite shapes help anchor beds and borders. For example, white loosestrife (*Lysimachia ephemerum*) keeps its columnar form through the summer and fall. Annual castor bean's (*Ricinus*) bold leaves and sturdy stems can serve as a focal point in a perennial border.

32 **Garden arches, sundials, benches, and birdbaths can also contribute structure to flower gardens.** Garden ornaments made of wood, metal, stone, and clay act as strong, crisp foils to soft-leaved plants. One birdbath or sundial can anchor a loosely structured island bed.

33 **Place your paths where they will be handiest for strolling around the garden.** Paths should be practical, allowing you to get easily from the street to the front door, from the back door into the garden, from the beds to the compost pile. Be sure you have paths where you need to move wheelbarrows and lawn mowers.

34 Let your paths contribute to the overall pattern of the garden. A gracefully winding path can flow through the garden, adding structural beauty through its shape and materials. A stone path makes the garden feel old and established. A brick or cobble path adds textural interest.

35 In the rainy areas of the Pacific Northwest, it's wise to avoid brick paths in the cooler, shadier parts of the garden. Brick paths in shade stay damp and can become treacherously slippery in the winter and spring. Exposed aggregate, crushed rock, or runner's bark will offer better traction.

COLOR

❀ ❀ ❀

36 **Pay attention to how different colors make you feel and select the ones that please you the most.** I love the color purple–to me it's regal and rich, but some people find it too intense. Red is exciting and enlivening to many gardeners, while others find it loud and irritating. Yellow can be perceived as cheerful or overpowering. Notice your own personal response and choose accordingly–the garden is a place for you to be happy.

37 **To create an exuberant mood and command attention, try a warm color scheme, combining red, yellow, and orange flowers.** Warm colors tend to jump forward toward the viewer, making the garden feel exciting, but also smaller. At the Bellevue Botanic Garden in Seattle, Washington, red *Crocosmia* 'Lucifer', orange pokers, dark red and yellow daylilies blend in a fiery composition. At Sissinghurst, red roses, yellow meadow rue (*Thalictrum speciosissimum*), red ladybug poppy (*Papaver commutatum*), and orange foxtail lilies (*Eremurus bungei*) mingle with high energy in the intimate cottage garden.

<38> **Keep red tinted with yellow separate from red tinted with blue.** Red containing yellow is a warm color and belongs with its kin—orange, yellow, and green that is more yellow than blue. Red containing blue is cooler and harmonizes better with similar companions—blue, lavender, purple, green with some blue in it.

<39> **Use gray foliage, creamy-white and blue flowers to mediate between clashing colors.** Blue-violet cranesbills *(Geranium himalayense)* cool down the war between my orange-red poppies and blue-red peonies that bloom too close for comfort every June. Similarly, gray *Artemisia* 'Powys Castle' and soft white Jupiter's beard *(Centranthus ruber* 'Alba') calm things down around my red, magenta, and pink shrub roses.

40 Select white and yellow flowers as a way of bringing sunshine into shady gardens. In Western Oregon and Western Washington, many gardens bloom beneath the canopy of native douglas firs and bigleaf maple. Add to that the naturally overcast winter and spring skies, and it's all too easy for the most avid gardener to get depressed. Color is the cure. In the recesses of shade and on gray days white and yellow show up best and lift the lowest spirits. A carpet of white snowdrops and yellow winter aconite illuminate the dark woodland floor in January. A group of yellow-green Corsican hellebores (*Helleborus corsicus*) and 'Tête-à-Tête' daffodils cheers my heart in February.

41 Remember that a painter's canvas is blank, but a gardener's canvas is green. Because most gardens have expanses of grass and foliage, green is the dominant color and must be taken into account in all color schemes. For example, a mass of red poppies is actually splashes of red on a backdrop of green leaves, perfect contrast of two complementary colors.

42 To make your garden appear bigger than it actually is, use the cooler colors: blue, violet, and

green. Cool colors tend to recede, and thus give the illusion of being further away from the eye. They are also more restful and create a mood of tranquillity, soothing the viewer.

◆43◆ Consider the size and shape of flowers and the way they're arranged on the plant when making color decisions. A double red rose such as 'Othello' has large, cupped flowers that stand out against green leaves, so the color effect is one of deep red accents against a green backdrop. This is relatively subtle, and pleasant for close-up viewing. A single red rose such as 'Red Coat' has wide-open red flowers nearly covering the shrub, thus forming a big block of red. This makes a strong impact, and is a great magnet from a distance.

◆44◆ Contrast big boldly shaped flowers with smaller sprays of flowers for a bouquet-like effect. Imagine a bouquet of roses and baby's breath, bold flowers set against delicate ones, and imitate this in the garden. The dainty white flowers of *Achillea declorans* 'W. B. Child' are a perfect foil for the double pink blooms of 'Mary Rose', an English reblooming shrub rose. Dark pink peonies with rounded flowers benefit from a carpet of *Gera-*

nium ibericum, with small blue flowers. Surround a favorite white rose with a froth of small pink-flowering cranesbills such as *Geranium endressii* 'Wargrave Pink' or *Geranium* x *oxonianum* 'A. T. Johnson'.

45 **If you're just starting out, pink, blue, and purple with a touch of white is sure to be pleasing.** If you look at a color wheel, you'll see that pink is a shade of red, and that red, blue, and purple are neighbors, making them very friendly to each other. Try pink tulips with blue forget-me-nots, purple aubretia, and white rock cress (*Arabis albida*) for spring, and pink roses with blue speedwell (*Veronica spicata*), purple larkspur, and white *Gaura lindheimerii* for summer.

46 **Pair red and white for a crisp, striking combination.** Red and white provide strong contrast and warmth. Plant red tulips with white 'Thalia' daffodils for springtime, and red 'Europeanna' or 'Scarlet Meidiland' shrub roses with white sweet alyssum or white cranesbills (*Geranium sanguineum* 'Album') for summer.

47 **Combine blue and yellow for a cheerful, welcoming feeling that reminds me of the sun's warmth**

in a blue sky. What could be more inviting than blue grape hyacinths and yellow daffodils in March? For June, try early yellow daylilies and blue Siberian iris, and yellow yarrow with blue balloon flowers for summer. Imagine yellow climbing roses accompanied by blue delphinium, yellow daisies (*Anthemis* 'Wargrave'), and blue Carpathian harebell (*Campanula carpatica*.)

48 **Dare to flaunt orange flowers, and combine them with blue or purple for the most electricity.** *Euphorbia griffithii* 'Fireglow' is assertive, but far from loud. Its orange bracts, maroon stems, and dark green tapered leaves fascinate visitors. Try it with deep purple 'Caesar's Brother' Siberian iris and orange sunrose (*Helianthemum* 'Henfield Brilliant'). I love orange Peruvian lilies (*Alstroemeria aurantiaca*) mixed with purple *Penstemon* 'Midnight Blue'.

49 **For a refined and harmonious garden, use many shades of one color. This is known as a monochromatic color scheme.** For spring, plant 50 or more tulips in shades of pink: pastel, medium pink, dark pink, and burgundy. Grow a stand of delphinium, blending shades of palest blue, sky blue, and navy. At Sissinghurst's white garden all the flowers are shades of white–creamy white, greenish white, chalk white. When the colors are so similar, the flower shapes become more noticeable. Foliage color and texture become more important too. Gray-leaved plants and a wide variety of textural differences–woolly leaves, crinkled leaves, pleated leaves–compensate for the simplicity of the color scheme.

◆**50** **To try out a new color scheme, make a bouquet of flowers that is pleasing, then create a garden picture with those plants.** One spring day I gathered a bouquet of blue hyacinths, and pink, apricot, and maroon tulips. For filler, I added a few stems of bishop's hat (*Epimedium sulphureum*), with sprays of delicate yellow flowers, and 'Arp' rosemary, covered with small blue flowers. To imitate this lovely bouquet in the garden, replicate the color scheme and also respect the horticultural needs of the plants. Place the rosemary in a sunny well-drained bed where it will thrive, with tulips and hyacinths in front of it. Plant shade-loving bishop's hat underneath a tree, with tulips and hyacinths out toward the drip line where they will get enough sun.

51 For longest lasting color in the garden, choose plants with unusual foliage: gold, gray, blue-green, and burgundy. Golden-leaved forms of ninebark, shrub honeysuckle (*Lonicera* 'Baggeson's Gold'), spiraea (*Spiraea* 'Goldflame'), barberry (*Berberis thunbergii* 'Aurea'), and elderberry (*Sambucus canadensis* 'Aurea') bring light and life to green borders. Gray-leaved lamb's ears, artemisia, and lavender flatter pink and orange flowers. Blue-green rue (*Ruta*), dusty meadow rue (*Thalictrum speciosissimum*), and hostas with bluish leaves (*Hosta sieboldiana*, *Hosta* 'Halcyon') add a soothing touch. The burgundy leaves of smoke tree (*Cotinus* 'Royal Purple'), purple barberry, and purple elderberry are rich foils for pink, blue, and orange flowers.

52 Place burgundy-leaved plants such as purple smoke tree, purple-leaved elderberry, purple-leaved barberry, and purple-leaved filbert where you want drama. Because their dark leaves contrast so strongly with green foliage, burgundy-leaved plants stand out and draw a lot of attention. They serve well as focal points in a mixed border, and should be used in moderate numbers since they carry more weight than green. To blend the burgundy leaves into the composition, grow flowers nearby with similar colors–spiny bear's breech (*Acanthus spinosus*), burgundy-colored 'Crossfield Ebony' dahlias, and dark red pincushion flower (*Knautia macedonica*.)

53 **Use variegated-leaved plants to create color echoes.** When you grow pink flowers near leaves that have pink variegation, the flower and foliage colors echo each other in a pleasing way. In shade, combine *Ajuga* 'Burgundy Glow', which has green, cream, and pink tones in its leaves, with pink primroses for spring, pink impatiens for summer, and pink autumn crocus (*Colchicum autumnale*). In sun, place purple sage near purple verbena for a summer color echo, or golden sage beside yellow-flowering *Coreopsis* 'Moonbeam'.

54 **Glossy green and golden foliage and leaves with white and cream-colored variegation illuminate shady places.** Japanese aralia's (*Fatsia japonica*) shiny green leaves bring light to the deepest shade. *Kerria japonica* 'Variegata' does the same with its variegated leaves and sweet yellow flowers. In dappled shade, golden elderberry and variegated elderberry introduce welcome brightness.

FLOWERING SHRUBS

55 **Plant tall flowering shrubs such as lilac and mock orange where you need backdrop for your perennial flower borders.** Tall shrubs do double duty by providing color during their bloom season and structural bones for the garden. Leave a few feet of space between the shrubs and the perennials so that you can get in to prune and fertilize.

56 **Choose shrubs with small and inconspicuous leaves to enhance the border flowers.** Avoid bold and shiny-leaved shrubs such as laurel or photinia when choosing shrubs for backdrop—they will detract from your flowers. Select subtler plants with dark green nonreflective leaves to support the showy perennials and annuals that bloom later.

57 **Use shrubs where you need walls to divide the garden into separate rooms.** Instead of fences, consider planting evergreen shrubs such as strawberry tree (*Arbutus unedo*), Japanese convexleaf holly (*Ilex crenata* 'Convexa'), or Mexican orange (*Choisya ternata*) as living walls.

58 **For a richer composition, add shrubs to thicken your flower borders.** A mixed border of shrubs, perennials, annuals, and bulbs will be more interesting and have a longer season of bloom than the traditional perennial border. 'Somerset' daphne, dwarf mock orange, dwarf lilac, and hybrid musk roses are excellent shrubs for the mixed border.

59 **Plant dwarf shrubs at the front of a border to create a strong finishing edge.** Often the front of a border is messy, especially when it's right next to the lawn. Grass creeps into the bed and weeds sneak in too. Dwarf shrubs make a thick barrier to keep these intruders out, while also providing a crisp visual boundary. Try dwarf

Japanese holly (*Ilex crenata* 'Helleri'), *Senecio greyi,* and dwarf lavender in sun. Variegated boxwood and dwarf sweet box *(Sarcococca hookeriana humilis)* are good choices for shade.

60 **Use evergreen shrubs where you most need permanent plantings.** Needle evergreens, also known as conifers, and broadleaf evergreens keep their leaves year-round. They're especially valuable in places you are likely to see in all seasons–the entry garden and beds in plain view of the kitchen and living room windows. Evergreens can also be planted to form permanent screening walls where you need privacy.

61 **For complete year-round privacy, a hedge of needle evergreens will do the trick.** Arborvitae, yew, incense cedar, and Canadian hemlock can be used to form dense green walls. Keep in mind that hedges take up 4 or more feet across and require regular clipping to look tidy. They contribute formality and strong lines to a garden.

62 **Use tall broadleaf evergreens for informal screening.** Choices abound for large sun-loving shrubs. *Co-*

toneaster lacteus and *Cotoneaster franchetii* have white spring flowers and a bonus of fall berries. Laurestinus *(Viburnum tinus)* has pink buds opening to lacy white flowers from fall through winter. Glossy abelia (*Abelia grandiflora*) has a profusion of late summer flowers on gracefully arching branches. In shade, use tall varieties of rhododendron, camellia, and andromeda–showy spring flowers brighten their dark leaves.

◇63◇ To have flowers in every season, grow a selection of deciduous shrubs. Many offer fragrance and decorative berries as well. From the earliest winter-blooming 'Dawn' viburnum to the red fall berries of winterberry (*Ilex verticillata*), deciduous shrubs give us reliable color for all seasons. While evergreen shrubs are steady, they are also static. Deciduous shrubs are more dynamic in their evolution from bare branches to flowers to fruit or fall color.

◇64◇ For the earliest bouquets, be sure to plant winter-blooming shrubs. Winter hazel (*Corylopsis*), wintersweet (*Chimonanthus*), and flowering quince are prized for their winter flowers, which are all the showier for blooming on bare branches. These are

large, spreading shrubs useful for backdrop, screening, or as part of a mixed
border.

**◆65◆ Spring is announced by for-
sythia and celebrated with lilac, mock orange, and daphne.** The
first bright yellow forsythia flowers give
us hope. Armloads of lilac for the house
make us feel wealthy. Mock orange,
daphne and lilac perfume home and
garden better than any potpourri.

**◆66◆ In sunny beds, roses give the
longest-lasting summer color.**
It's hard to beat the reblooming roses
for flowers and fragrance. The difficulty
is narrowing down the choices—there
are Bourbons, rugosas, hybrid
perpetuals, hybrid musks, English roses,
shrub roses, hybrid teas, grandifloras,
floribundas, polyanthas, miniatures,
and patio roses to tempt you. Check ul-
timate heights and widths for intelligent
placement, using bigger shrubs for
backdrop and screening, medium-size
plants for mid-border, and small ones
in the foreground.

**◆67◆ Rugosa roses, also called sea to-
matoes, are the toughest roses
for impenetrable hedges.** Their bright
green pleated leaves, fragrant flowers,
and shiny red fruit, rich in vitamin C,

more than compensate for their wicked thorns. Happiest in sandy soils and perfect for coastal gardens, they nevertheless grow satisfactorily in my clay soil.

◆68◆ Hybrid musk roses are good candidates for mixed borders and also thrive in partial shade. Repeat-flowering hybrid musks bloom in clusters of small but profuse flowers, allowing them to blend companionably with perennials and annuals. Unlike the stiff-caned hybrid tea roses, hybrid musks have more relaxed branches and spread wider than they grow tall. Use them toward the back or middle of the border to thicken the planting and provide lots of color in summer and fall.

◆69◆ In sunny places, grow butterfly bushes (*Buddleia davidii*) for long-lasting summer color, heady perfume, and places for butterflies to picnic. Buddleias come in wide color selections–pink, dark purple, blue, lavender, magenta, white, even orangey-yellow. Growing rapidly to 8 feet tall, they are wonderful screens where you need summer privacy. My favorites are 'Lochinch', with gray leaves and lavender flowers, 'Royal Red', with brilliant red-purple flowers, and 'Purple Prince'.

70 In shady borders, hydrangeas are best bets for summer color. Hydrangeas bloom in shades of pink, blue, and white, forming medium to large shrubs that look best in groups. Mop-headed and lace-cap forms of hydrangea are most commonly available, but it is worth the effort to seek out the more unusual species. Oak-leaf hydrangea (*Hydrangea quercifolia*) has creamy white flowers and elegant leaves that turn red in the fall if grown in morning sun. *Hydrangea serrata* 'Preziosa' has flowers with tints of pink, red, and lavender, dark leaves, and burgundy stems. Majestic in stature, *Hydrangea aspera* 'Villosa' has velvety leaves and lacy flowers in shades of mauve and lavender.

71 Plant hardy fuchsias in shady areas where you want lots of summer color and a subtle composition. Hardy fuschias are upright, deciduous shrubs that grow 3 to 5 feet tall, with tons of narrow tubular flowers that drape gracefully from the branches. There are pink, red, and white varieties. In early spring, cut the woody stems down to ground level, and they'll return stronger than ever. A 4-foot-tall hedge of red-flowering hardy fuchsias makes a spectacular summer sight.

72 **Variegated shrubs introduce light into shade gardens.** Like an impressionist watercolor, the leaves of *Fuchsia magellanica* 'Versicolor' blend shades of gray, rose-pink, and cream, inviting closer attention. Its flowers are red and purple. *Hydrangea macrophylla* 'Variegata' has leaves edged with cream, and blue flowers. Spectacular *Hydrangea macrophylla* 'Quadricolor' has foliage of pale green, cream, deep green, and yellow, and lilac flowers.

73 **Include fruiting shrubs for fall and winter interest.** *Rosa glauca*, *Rosa moyesii* 'Geranium', and *Rosa rugosa* set showy red hips that brighten the fall and winter garden. 'Profusion' beautyberry (*Callicarpa bodinieri* 'Profusion') forms clusters of bright violet berries in the fall–I cut clusters and tuck them into Christmas wreaths. Every winter I stop to admire a neighborhood hedge of *Cotoneaster lacteus* full of handsome red berries.

74 **Go out on a limb and try some novelty shrubs for fun.** New shrub cultivars abound, with interesting leaves, flowers, and fruit. In sun, try *Hypericum* x *inodorum* 'Elstead', a beauty for the summer garden, covered with yellow flowers that show their matching stamens. These form pinkish-red berries that darken to black by fall. *Hypericum androsaemum* 'Albury Purple' has rich coppery foliage. *Sorbaria arborea* makes a nice tall accent in shade. White flower plumes top its ferny leaves in summer.

CHOICE PERENNIALS

75 **Think of perennials when you're looking for colorful carpets in front of your trees and shrubs.** Perennials provide flowers that return every year, and bloom anywhere from 2 weeks to several months. Use them in masses to dress up the front of your beds. In the shade, group astilbes and hostas in front of rhododendrons and camellias. In sun, mass daylilies in mixed orange and yellow tones forward of yellow-flowering shrub St. Johnswort (*Hypericum* 'Hidcote') for a cheering summer picture.

76 **Use perennials with long bloom periods in summer and fall near patios and seating areas.** Put your seasonal color where you can most enjoy it, close to where you sit. Combine red and yellow blanket flower (*Gaillardia grandiflora*), yellow yarrow (*Achillea* x *taygetea*), and red *Crocosmia* 'Lucifer' for a sunny composition. If you prefer cooler colors plant a trio of pink evening primrose (*Oenothera speciosa*), lavender Russian sage (*Perovskia atriplicifolia*), and pink hollyhock mallow (*Malva alcea* 'Fastigiata').

77 **Grow perennials that last well for indoor bouquets.** There are too many to list, but here are my top favorites. For spring: peonies, cottage pinks (*Dianthus plumarius*), lady's mantle (*Alchemilla mollis*), blue speedwell (*Veronica*), Jupiter's beard (*Centranthus ruber*), peach-leaf bellflower (Campanula persicifolia). For summer: *Aster* x *frikartii* and feverfew (*Chrysanthemum parthenium*), especially the double white form. Also balloon flower (*Platycodon grandiflorus)*, gooseneck loosestrife (*Lysimachia clethroides*), fringed yellow loosestrife (*Lysimachia ciliata*), Peruvian lily (*Alstroemeria aurantiaca*), purple coneflower (*Echinacea purpurea*), perennial pincushion flower (*Scabiosa caucasica*), masterwort (*Astrantia major*). For fall: kaffir lily (*Schizostylis coccinea*), obedience plant

(*Physostegia virginiana*), and the delicate species aster, *Aster ericoides*, with tiny white flowers.

78 **For longer-lasting bouquets, cut flowers between 8 P.M. and 8 A.M.** Since high temperatures can stress flowers, it's best to harvest them when it's cool, late in the evening or early in the morning. Take a bucket of cold water with you and strip off the lower leaves before immersing the stems (to prevent bacterial growth). Arrange the stems loosely for good air circulation. Recut stems under water to prevent air bubbles from blocking the upward flow of water. Store containers of cut flowers in a cool place such as a basement for a few hours to condition the blooms.

79 **Include perennials with long bloom periods in containers for added interest.** Give yourself more color and texture by combining perennials with annuals. Choose perennials that stand on their own feet without stakes–*Penstemon* 'Midnight Blue', yellow *Coreopsis* 'Moonbeam', and the more compact form of *Aster* x *frikartii*, 'Jungfrau'. Blue oat grass (*Helictotrichon sempervirens*) and 'Jackman's Blue' rue make great foliage accents in containers.

80 Use perennials to fill in the gaps while your shrubs grow to their mature size. When I began my garden I relied on *Geranium pratense*, a blue-violet hardy cranesbill, to cover the ground between young shrubs in a big border. It spread by root and seed with an ocean of blue flowers in early summer, and choked out the lower-growing weeds. *Geranium pratense* is a strong grower that tolerates heavy clay soil, and I've selectively removed it as the shrubs and choicer perennials have filled in.

81 Attractive leaves are as important as flowers when you select perennials for your garden. Perennials bloom for weeks, but their leaves are key elements for months. Notice the variation in leaf shapes; for example, rounded lady's mantle (*Alchemilla mollis*), lacy meadow rue (*Thalictrum*), and linear, bladelike iris. Create interesting combinations by contrasting round leaves with linear ones, lacy leaves with broader neighbors.

82 Rounded, lobed, and broad leaves are especially valuable at the border's edge to anchor the composition. *Bergenia, Geranium renardii, Geranium nudosum, Geranium himalayense, Galax aphylla,* hostas, and coral bells (*Heuchera*) have nicely shaped leaves that are bold enough to frame the front of a border. Use a generous number of the same plant to define the edge adequately, especially if you want to accentuate a curve.

83 **Lacy-leaved plants make good fillers between perennials with bolder leaves.** I like to plant ferns, astilbe, columbines, and meadow rue (*Thalictrum*) between clumps of more dramatic *Hosta*, *Ligularia*, and *Rodgersia*. The showier leaves are the stars, the subtler ones act as supporting players.

84 **Choose perennials with definite shapes to give a feeling of order to the border.** *Lysimachia ephemerum*, a white-flowering loosestrife with dark gray-green leaves, forms a striking 4-foot column. Set among billowing masses of pink and blue cranesbills (*Geranium*), the loosestrife stands upright with steady, reassuring strength. One such accent here and there has a calming effect on a busy border. Cushion spurge (*Euphorbia polychroma*), a low mound covered with bright yellow bracts in springtime, serves well as an anchor at the front of a sunny border. Its rounded shape contrasts well with vertical stems of Siberian iris.

85 **Give priority to perennials that bloom for 10 weeks or more to get the most color into your borders.** Some perennials have fleeting flowers, which are here and gone within 2 weeks. This is fine in a large garden, but in a smaller space, capitalize on color by choosing the plants that flower longer. Perennial pincushion flower (*Scabiosa caucasica*), *Aster* x *frikartii*, purple coneflower (*Echinacea purpurea*), *Coreopsis* 'Moonbeam', *Gaura lindheimerii*, 'Stella de Oro' daylily, 'Happy Returns' daylily, and *Penstemon* 'Midnight Blue' are just a few perennials that bloom for most of the summer and fall.

86 **Avoid invasive perennials— those that run rapidly by underground roots or seed down mercilessly.** Stay away from rampant plants unless you have a very large garden, for they will overtake your more moderate growers and consume hours of weeding time. Catalogues will describe them as "vigorous" or "strong," which are simply euphemisms for pests. Some examples: forget-me-not, feverfew, bugleweed (*Ajuga reptans*), bishop's weed (*Aegopodium* *podagraria*), ribbon grass (*Phalaris arundinacea*), yellow loosestrife (*Lysimachia punctata*), *Euphorbia cyparissias*, most bearded iris, yellow flag iris (*Iris pseudacorus*), *Geranium* 'Claridge Druce', and periwinkle (*Vinca minor*). Of course these plants can be grown beneficially as ground cover where little else will grow.

87 **Be sure to include perennials that bloom in each season to ensure year-round color in your garden.** For winter, Christmas, Lenten, Corsican, and bearsfoot hellebores (*Helleborus niger, H. orientalis, H. corsicus, H. foetidus*) are musts. *Pulmonaria* 'Roy Davidson' begins flowering in February and goes on past Mother's Day. Plant evergreen candytuft, aubretia, creeping phlox, wallflowers, tulips, and daffodils for spring starters. Peonies, cranesbills, daylilies, bellflowers, iris, and astilbes will see you safely into early summer. Follow up with Frikart's asters, coneflowers, speedwells, later daylilies, later cranesbills, summer phlox, balloon flowers, mallows, lavender, Russian sage, and *Coreopsis* for mid-summer mainstays. Late summer 'Mount Fuji' phlox, obedience plant, and 'Goldsturm' black-eyed Susan carry the color into fall. Add Michaelmas daisies, sneezeweed (*Helenium*), kaffir lily

(*Schizostylis coccinea*), and fall-flowering sedums (*Sedum spectabile, Sedum sieboldii, Sedum* 'Vera Jameson') for a grand finale.

‹88› **Remove spent flowers to keep perennials attractive.** Daylilies, tickweed (*Coreopsis*), Shasta daisies, and peach-leaved bellflower are just a few of the perennials that produce so many flowers for such a long time that the spent, browned flowers can ruin the plant's overall beauty. Deadheading is gardener's jargon for pinching off the dead flowers. This makes a remarkable improvement in a plant's appearance, allowing the fresh flowers to shine. Be careful not to remove new buds by accident.

‹89› **To prevent legginess and eliminate the need for staking, cut back tall, late-blooming perennials in the spring.** Michaelmas daisies, chrysanthemums, boltonia, and sneezeweed (*Helenium*) tend to become lanky. Wait until they've grown up to about 3 feet tall in late spring, then prune them back to a foot. This will thicken the plants by forcing them to branch out more at the base.

90 **To prevent spring-blooming perennials that drape and spill
from becoming stringy, cut them back
after they've finished flowering.** Cottage pinks (*Dianthus plumarius*), rock
cress (*Aubretia deltoidea*), basket-of-
gold (*Aurinia saxatilis*), evergreen
candytuft (*Iberis sempervirens*), and
snow-in-summer (*Cerastium
tomentosum*) all benefit from a radical
pruning in early summer. Just grab their
stems in one hand and cut them as if
you were giving them a short haircut,
leaving about 2 inches at the base. The
stems will branch out and produce fresh
foliage for the summer garden.

91 **Some perennials can be cut
down to the ground after
blooming, and will produce new leaves
and bloom a second time.** By experi-
menting I have discovered that lady's
mantle (*Alchemilla mollis*), globe thistle
(*Echinops ritro*), and spiderwort (*Tradescantia virginiana*) can be cut clear
back to the ground after their flowers
and leaves become shabby. I've gotten
two and even three surges of growth
and bloom from these plants by radical
pruning. I've cut back Corsican hellebores when their leaves have been
damaged by cold, and oriental poppies
after they've bloomed–their leaves turn
yellow-brown–but neither rebloom.

They do, however, produce new attractive foliage.

92 **Stake perennials with heavy flowers that need support.** Peonies, spiderwort, and the taller cranesbills such as *Geranium magnificum* tend to fall over and collapse in our heavy spring and summer rain. Prevention is the best cure. In early spring, just as the plants are emerging from the ground, surround them with brushy prunings from your fruit trees. Insert these twiggy branches in the ground and let them buttress your floppier plants. By the time the perennials grow up, this underpinning will be totally hidden beneath expanding foliage.

93 **Place low hedges of sturdy lavender or dwarf boxwood at the front of your perennial border to support the more billowy plants behind them.** At Powys Castle in Wales the dwarf boxwood hedges keep spiderwort (*Tradescantia virginiana*) and peonies from falling on their faces. In my garden a low hedge of *Coreopsis* 'Moonbeam' contains the billowing bright pink 'Russell Pritchard' and 'Cedric Morris' cranesbills.

94 **Plant later-blooming perennials between those plants that go dormant in the summer.** Oriental poppy (*Papaver orientale*) and bleeding heart (*Dicentra spectabile*) are showy in the spring but die down to the ground in the summer, leaving gaps in beds and borders. To fill the spaces, plant perennials beside them that leaf out and flower later. In sun, plant daylilies, obedience plant (*Physostegia virginiana*) or *Aster* x *frikartii* near oriental poppies. Their leaves will arise as the poppies foliage goes dormant. In shade, plant astilbes, ferns, or willow gentians (*Gentiana asclepiadea*) near bleeding heart to camouflage its yellowing leaves.

ANNUALS AND BIENNIALS

95 **Wait until May 15 to plant annuals in the Pacific Northwest.** Although we get spring fever and annuals are offered for sale as early as March, little is gained by planting them sooner than May 15. Cool soil, cold nights, continuous rain, and occasional hail often kills annuals planted prematurely. At the best petunias, zinnias, impatiens, and marigolds will sit there sulking until the weather warms up.

96 **If you simply can't wait to plant flowers, cool-weather annuals and biennials and are safe to plant as**

46

early as February and March. You can get away with planting pansies, stock, nemesia, calendula, wallflowers, snapdragons, geraniums, and sweet alyssum while the weather is still cool and uncertain.

◆ **97** **Take advantage of annuals where you need steady summer color.** Plant annuals where you spend time in summer—near patios, swimming pools, porches, and decks. Since they bloom for only one year, they put their heart and soul into flowering, offering us continuous summer color in a diversity of hues.

◆ **98** **Biennials too offer steady summer color, but not until their second year. They sprout and form leaves during their first season, bloom the following year, then set seed and die.** Foxgloves, sweet William, Miss Wilmott's ghost (*Eryngium giganteum*), and cardoon are just a few of the intriguing biennials that tease us the first year with their leaves and reward us with a bounty of flowers the second year. Most biennials self-sow, making them perennial for all practical purposes. Just be sure to leave a few spent flower stems so that seed will form and disperse to renew their 2-year cycle. Where winters are mild, biennials may live longer than two years, defying their definition.

99 **Plant annuals and biennials to fill in gaps while your shrubs and perennials mature.** Annuals and biennials give you instant color and keep out undesirable weeds in the spaces between the more permanent plants that need time to develop. They are the reward you need for being patient while your garden slowly grows up.

100 **For a more natural-looking garden, plant annuals in small groups.** Victorian gardens popularized bedding out, or planting annuals in big blocks of primary colors—red salvia, blue lobelia, white alyssum. Parks and commercial landscapes favor this dazzling look, which can appear garish in small residential gardens. Combine smaller drifts of annuals for a subtle, harmonious picture.

101 **Be sure to plant sweet William (*Dianthus barbatus*), sweet alyssum (*Lobularia maritima*), and sweet peas (*Lathyrus odoratus*), flowers so beloved for their fragrance.** Sweet William, a biennial, is easily grown from seed scattered on well-prepared soil. Its heads of pink, red, white, and patterned flowers perfume the garden and cut well for bouquets. At the feet of roses and perennials it's a perfect cottage-garden edger. Sweet alyssum's delicate white or pink flowers add old-fashioned charm. It's especially useful in small spaces, even crevices. And sweet peas are cherished for remembrance of grandmother's garden and cut flowers.

102 **Seek out the unusual scented annuals for fun.** Heliotrope (*Heliotropium arborescens*), chocolate cosmos (*Cosmos atrosanguineum*), and woodland tobacco (*Nicotiana sylvestris*) are my three favorites. Heliotrope's lacy flower heads, purple, lavender, or white, fill the air with vanilla. I like them mixed in containers or at the front of the border, the better to sniff. Chocolate cosmos is as appealing for its scent as for its burgundy-red flowers—they look like miniature dahlias. Woodland tobacco, with bold tropical-looking leaves and white flower trumpets, perfume the evening garden.

103 **Plant novelty annuals and biennials for their striking foliage and surprising flowers.** Cardoon (*Cynara cardunculus*), often mistaken for an artichoke, has enormous gray leaves that are boldly jagged. By summer it is 6 feet tall with thistlelike buds that open to pinkish-purple flowers in July. The burgundy-leaved form of castor bean plant (*Ricinus communis*) has exotic hand-shaped flowers on thick, succulent stems. In late summer red flower spikes jazz up the tall dramatic plant. Spiny seedpods form in the fall, containing deadly seeds, which should be removed if young children are around. Castor bean plant looks equally handsome at the back of a border and in a large pot. So does princess flower (*Tibouchena urvilleana*), a furry-leaved shrubby annual with vivid purple flowers the size of a silver dollar.

⟨104⟩ Plant a wall of tall annuals where you need quick summer screening, in front of a plain fence, or at the back of a deep border. Cosmos and spider flower (*Cleome hassleriana*) add height in a hurry to new borders. Since both self-sow, I count on them to fill the gaps while the tall shrubs and perennials fill in. Cosmos has lacy leaves and anemone-like flowers in shades of pink and white. Similar in color, cleome's flowers are in clusters with long thin stamens that look like whiskers. Its leaves are hand-shaped.

105 For a sunny, bold accent, try some tall tithonias and sunflowers. Large furry leaves and bright orange flowers in late summer make tithonia, also known as Mexican sunflower, a standout. Similarly sunflowers (*Helianthus annua*), especially hybrids like 'Italian White', 'Red Sun', and 'Moonwalker', contribute joie de vivre to the garden. Add tall dahlias and cannas in hot colors—orange, red, or yellow—for a fiery statement.

106 Love-lies-bleeding (*Amaranthus caudatus*) makes a unique garden sculpture in a border or container. Rising five feet tall and spreading wider, with long velvety red flower tassels that drape, love-lies-bleeding is an irresistible curiosity piece. I saw it in a country garden underplanted with billowing thyme; in an estate garden combined with white fall anemones (*Anemone japonica*) and 'Autumn Joy' sedums. 'Viridis' has long green tassels, and 'Pigmy Torch', on my wish list, has deep maroon upright spikes like many gigantic fingers pointing to the sky.

107 Mix some green-flowering annuals into your borders for a subtle touch. *Nicotiana* 'Lime Green', a pale green flowering tobacco hybrid, is fun to mix into flower borders. I like it near variegated privet and creamy-white masterwort (*Astrantia major*) in shade. Equally unusual, *Nicotiana langsdorfii* has narrow flower bells that sway gracefully on slender stems. Bells of Ireland's (*Moluccella laevis*) flowers face out of long spires, looking a bit ghostly among their brighter-colored companions. *Zinnia* 'Envy' offers this same pale green. I once saw a sunny border that mixed these green flowers with blues and yellows very effectively. I like green equally well with magenta.

◇108◇ Pinch back the main stem to about six inches on zinnias, marigolds, cosmos, dahlias, cleome, and coleus, for better-branched plants. Often annuals are sold as single-stemmed plants with one flower blooming at the tip. If you sacrifice that first flower and cut the plant back, leaving about 6 inches of old growth, the annual will renew itself by branching out where you have pruned it. This produces a stockier plant with many more flowering stems.

◇109◇ Replace tatty-looking self-sowers with annuals that bloom a little later in the summer. I love foxgloves when they bloom in June beside the old roses, but once their flowers are spent and their leaves begin to yellow, I pull most of them out, leaving just a few to set seed. I plant *Nicotiana sylvestris* and larkspur in the gaps that remain.

110 **Keep self-sowing annuals under control by removing all but a few of their seedpods before they ripen. Thin out excess seedlings in the spring.** *Verbena bonariensis*, pot marigold (*Calendula*), Shirley poppies, foxglove, love-in-a-mist, flowering tobacco (*Nicotiana alata*), cosmos, and spider flower (*Cleome*) seed so readily that they can easily become pests. To restrain them, remove most of their seedpods in late summer before they have a chance to ripen and scatter. In spring, keep an eye out for seedlings and weed out the surplus. To do this accurately take time to learn the shape of each annual's new leaves.

111 **When it comes to annuals, it's especially important to remove their spent flowers to prevent them from setting seed.** Annuals will look better when deadheaded and will also bloom longer. Once they begin to form seed they have insured themselves for future seasons and lose their incentive to flower.

112 To save seed for future years, collect seedpods on a dry day, and save them in paper bags. Seeds stay dry best in paper–they tend to mold and mildew when damp, especially when stored in plastic containers. Write the plant's name and the date on the paper bag. Store the bags in a cool, dark place to keep the seeds fresh.

BULBS

113 **Plant bulbs for early color to jump-start the season.** Small blue stars bloom in my garden as early as January. Glory-of-the-snow (*Chionodoxa luciliae*) is only 6 inches tall and best planted in groups of at least 25, near a doorway that you use in winter. If you have well-drained soil, add a dozen netted iris (*Iris reticulata*) for an elegant winter surprise. Their velvety blue flowers are brightened by small yellow tongues.

114 **Try a tapestry of bulbs for winter ground cover.** You can have a garden bright with color as early as New Year's Day. Plant groups of yellow winter aconite (*Eranthis hyemalis*) and lavender crocus beneath winter-flowering shrubs such as the 'Dawn' viburnum (*Viburnum bodnantense* 'Dawn') or yellow witch hazel (*Hamamelis mollis*.)

115 **Many bulbs are drought tolerant and make excellent woodland carpets to brighten Pacific Northwest woodlands.** Plant bulbs in areas that get rain and light in winter but go dry in summer, for example beneath the canopy of deciduous trees. Groups of white snowdrops (*Galanthus nivalis*) planted behind splashes of fuschia-pink winter cyclamen (*Cyclamen coum*) make a striking picture in February. Winter cyclamen is perfectly hardy, and drought-tolerant. Glossy leaves marbled with silver and small, brilliant flowers that bloom super-early make it a standout.

116 **Plant the earliest daffodils for winter color.** 'February Gold' and 'Tête-à-Tête' are bright yellow daffodils that open in February. I love them combined with masses of blue *Pulmonaria* 'Roy Davidson', which flowers at the same time and keeps going until May. 'Minnow' and 'Jack Snipe' are also very early bloomers, both white with yellow centers. 'Jetfire' is a vivid daffodil, its long orange central trumpet surrounded by egg-yolk-yellow petals that recurve backward. Most of these early bloomers are short (8 inches or so) and are often listed as rock garden bulbs in catalogues–many are hybrids of *Narcissus cyclamineus*.

117 **For intense fragrance, choose Jonquilla, Tazetta, Triandrus, and Poeticus hybrid daffodils.** Jonquils are noted for their delicious scent. 'Baby Moon,' a pale yellow miniature, bright yellow 'Lintie', and taller (18") lemon-yellow 'Trevithian' are all beauties. Paperwhites for indoor forcing are the best known Tazetta daffodils; for the garden, try vibrant 'Geranium', with orange cups and creamy-white petals. Triandrus hybrids are very graceful, with recurved petals on nodding flowers. Examples are pure white 'Thalia', known as the "orchid narcissus," and yellow 'Hawera', a miniature perfect for rock gardens. Taller (16") 'Actea', pure white with a yellow cup edged in red, is a striking Poeticus hybrid.

118 **Jonquilla, Tazetta, and Triandrus hybrid daffodils produce many flowers per stem.** Blooming in clusters of 2 to 6 flowers on each stem, these hybrids give you more flowers per stem and a longer flowering period than the single- flowering trumpet daffodils. They are wonderful for bouquets.

119 **Select hyacinths for early color and fragrance.** Hyacinths add pink, blue, and white to the color choices and scent the garden in late winter and early spring. Alone they look thick and blocky. Help them out by planting taller daffodils behind them and pansies or primroses in related colors at their feet.

120 **Experiment with the charming species tulips where you need early color.** Species tulips, also known as wild or botanical tulips, are the first of their kind to bloom in early spring. Low to the ground, they withstand wind and rain storms better than the taller hybrids. They look best in rock gardens or circling trees—they are too small for big borders. My favorite is red and white *Tulipa clusiana*, the peppermint stick tulip.

121 **Plant tulips where the soil is dry in summer.** Tulips are native to habitats with little summer rain and are likely to rot if planted in beds that are watered regularly. Your best bet is to plant them at the base of trees where the soil is dry during the summer, in well-drained rock gardens or banks, or in areas of the garden that aren't irrigated.

122 **Plant tender bulbs as surprises in containers.** Peacock orchid (*Acidanthera bicolor*) sends up mysterious green spears in summer. In August, fragrant white flowers with maroon centers create a stir. When visitors ask "What is it?" you can reply with a smile, *"Acidanthera!"* I like it with chocolate cosmos, a wine-colored annual that echoes the peacock orchid's center.

123 **Blue lily-of-the-Nile (*Agapanthus orientalis*) is a welcome summer accent in pots.** Although tender, this bulb has such showy globes of blue flowers that I am willing to grow them in pots and winter them over in the basement. I place these containers in parts of the border that need tall focal points.

124 **Use summer bulbs to add color to beds and borders.** Three-foot-tall wands of red flower sprays make *Crocosmia* 'Lucifer' a smashing mid-border plant in July. It lures hummingbirds out of the hawthorn trees. When I hear their high-pitched chatter I tiptoe over to watch them. First they hover like mini-helicopters, then they dip and dive into the red flowers, probing for nectar. A cousin of 'Lucifer', *Crocosmia* 'Solfatare' has chocolate-colored leaves and apricot-yellow flowers. It's lovely with daylilies, dahlias, and yarrows in pastel shades of yellow and orange.

125 **Dahlias, although not reliably hardy, are valuable bulbs for late summer and autumn.** I rely on pink 'Park Princess', a 2-foot-tall border cactus dahlia, for long-lasting color without staking in the middle of my pink and purple bed. 'Crossfield Ebony', a wine-colored pompom dahlia, is super to create color echoes near purple barberries, purple smoketree, or *Hydrangea* 'Preziosa'. 'Edinburgh', a white and maroon bicolor dahlia, is also effective near purple-leaved plants.

126 **Try some flowering onions (*Allium* species and hybrids) for fun.** Most flowering onions have the same globe-shaped flowers as leeks, onions, garlic, and chives. My favorite, 'Purple Sensation', is true to its name. Large purple flower heads bloom at the tops of 3-foot-tall sturdy stems. I love a half dozen grouped behind blue columbines or in front of the sulfur-yellow spurge (*Euphorbia palustris*) that blooms in mid-spring. *Allium neapolitanum* has graceful clusters of white flowers in late spring when the old roses begin to bloom. Alliums prefer a rich, well-drained soil. Their flowers can be cut or dried. Left out in the garden, flowering onions fade to a beige color, remaining texturally interesting all summer and fall.

◆127◆ **Plant fall-flowering bulbs to extend the season.** Autumn crocus (*Colchicum autumnale* and *Colchicum speciosum*), also called meadow saffron, are showy when planted in groups of at least five. In spring they produce long leaves that turn yellow and die back by summer. In the fall, spectacular pink or white flowers bloom on naked stems. To ameliorate this unusual growth pattern, place autumn crocus beside a plant with permanent leaves. Try the pink-flowering autumn crocus beside *Geranium macrorrhizum*, with low-growing evergreen foliage. The white autumn crocus (*Colchicum speciosum* 'Album') looks handsome beside the marbled silvery leaves of hardy cyclamen.

◆128◆ **For the best impact plant bulbs in groups big enough to make a splash of color.** Books tell you to try for a natural effect by throwing bulbs over your shoulder and planting them where they land. The results are neither natural nor satisfying. Even in the wild, plants tend to grow in colonies, and certainly in the garden where we use plants to paint colorful compositions, groups of bulbs make stronger pictures. Dig one ample hole that is twice as deep as the thickness of your bulbs and big enough for a dozen or so bulbs. Take the dirt that you've removed from the hole and break it up with a spade until it is crumbly and loose. Then smooth out the bottom of the hole so that it is level, sprinkle it with bonemeal, set your bulbs at the bottom, a few inches apart, and cover them all at once with the crumbly dirt. Water them well and wait with joyful anticipation.

129 **When in doubt about which end of a bulb is up, simply plant it on its side and it will right itself.** Many bulbs have roots at their base which tell you which end is down, but some bulbs are more mysteriously egg-shaped or irregular, with no hint of roots or heads pointing upward. Place these sideways and they will right themselves as the roots begin to grow downwards.

130 **Always mark your bulbs with a label or a low stake so that you don't accidentally dig into them later on in the summer when their foliage disappears.** More than once I have begun to make a planting hole in summer only to discover that I was slicing right through a group of daffodils. Whoops! It's best to mark your plantings–white plastic labels break and look conspicuous, so I use low twigs that blend into the dirt yet remind my shovel that there are bulbs down there.

131 **The easiest way to plant bulbs without disturbing them is beneath a loose-growing ground cover of perennials.** Plant drifts of bulbs between clumps of hosta, bishop's hat (*Epimedium*), or lady's mantle (*Alchemilla mollis*) in the shade; between cranesbills (*Geranium*) or daylilies in the sun. When the bulbs have finished flowering, as their leaves turn yellow and die, the nearby perennials will fill in to cover up the mess.

132 **Groups of bulbs are useful between the crowns of perennials that leaf out in late spring and early summer.** *Aster* x *frikartii* and Russian sage (*Perovskia*) are good examples of plants that billow out by July but occupy only a small amount of ground in spring when their new leaves emerge. Use that empty space around them to enjoy the early bulbs. The perennials will provide the next surge of bloom when the bulbs die back.

133 **The best time to cut back the dying foliage on bulbs is 6 weeks after they bloom.** Controlled experiments conducted by Cornell University have shown that cutting back the dying foliage on bulbs any sooner than 6 weeks after they bloom lessens their flowering in future years. Waiting any longer makes no difference. The ripening foliage returns energy to the bulb for use the next year.

134 **Sow annuals and biennials that germinate easily beside bulbs to cover their dying foliage.** An easy way to fill in the gaps around bulbs that are through blooming is to spread a few inches of finished compost around the foliage that you have cut back. Water the compost well first, then sprinkle seed lightly over the top (that way you won't wash away your seed). Red flax (*Linum rubrum*), with shiny red flowers above ferny leaves, sweet William, and love-in-a-mist all start readily.

CONTAINER GARDENING

135 **Fill your containers with rich, well-draining potting soil for the best results.** Since potted plants grow in small quarters for a relatively short time, conditions should be ideal to help them develop and bloom quickly. A dark, crumbly soil containing compost or peat moss will hold enough moisture to keep the plants happy without getting waterlogged.

136 **Make sure that your container has enough drainage holes to let excess water run through.** Whether your pot is made of clay, wood, plastic, or metal, there must be a way for surplus water to drain. If there aren't adequate drainage holes, drill several.

If that's impossible, fill the bottom of your container with at least 6 inches of gravel or pottery shards—extra water can collect in this well.

137 **Fill the bottom of very large pots with styrofoam peanuts to keep your pots lightweight.** Big containers are often 3 feet tall, and annual roots rarely grow deeper than a foot. Pots filled with damp soil can get very heavy—by filling the bottom layer with Styrofoam, your pots will be lighter and easier to move.

138 **Remember to water your containers regularly and thoroughly.** Consistent, generous watering is the most important step for growing healthy container plants. Make sure to water pots until you see surplus water leaving the drainage holes. A hose-end watering wand makes it easy to reach into pots and delivers a gentle spray. In the Pacific Northwest summers can be very dry, and daily watering is crucial, especially in terra cotta pots and hanging baskets. On very hot or windy days pots should be watered twice.

139 **Use a combination of slow-release granular fertilizer and liquid supplements to develop healthy**

plants and sustain flowering. I mix Osmocote liberally into the potting soil at planting time—this is a balanced plant food that releases nutrients slowly during the growing season. Then I alternately apply liquid Miracle-Gro, Rapid Gro, and Bloom Plus every couple of weeks to give the plants a boost.

140 **Choose big pots for the showiest results; group smaller pots together for the best impact.** To have enough space for an ample display, containers must be at least 18 inches in diameter. Two-or three-foot-wide pots will be even more sumptuous-looking. If you have many small pots, group them together for a stronger picture.

141 **Stuff your pots full of plants for a plush bouquet.** Annuals grow for one season only—to get a quick start for early enjoyment buy the biggest plants available and plant them shoulder to shoulder in your pots. Individual pots and cell-pack annuals will also transplant more easily than tray-packs, making their extra cost pay off in terms of even, uninterrupted growth. Although tray-packs are more economical, to divide plants within them you must tear their root systems—this shocks them and slows them down.

142 Think of a free-standing container as a large flower arrangement: place taller plants toward the middle of the pot, drapers beside the rim, and intermediate fillers in between. One favorite combination in sun is African daisy (*Osteospermum*) toward the center, Swan River daisy trailing over the edge, and heliotrope sandwiched in between. In shade I like upright fuchsias in the center, lobelia trailing over the rim, and impatiens filling in between them.

143 Place containers where you will notice them most and close to a water bib for easy maintenance. Porches, patios, and decks are high-traffic places where you and your guests will be sure to enjoy containers. Make your life easier by placing containers near water sources—dragging hoses or sprinkling cans long distances in summer's heat is unnecessary work.

144 Wide staircases are opportunities for staging pots. If you have a staircase ample enough for people and pots, dress it up with colorful containers at the edges. Fragrant annuals like heliotrope, chocolate cosmos, scented geraniums, lemon verbena, and pineapple sage are especially welcome where passersby can brush up beside them.

145 **Window boxes can dress up the front of your house and make a garden shed look like a small cottage.** Window box flowers put the color at eye level where you can most appreciate it. They add a touch of old-fashioned charm, and a sense of welcome. By attaching window boxes to a garden shed or the side of a garage, you can create the illusion of a small house, perhaps for special guests. Train a clematis up the side for a finishing touch. It's the details that make a garden interesting.

146 **Tree limbs, arbors, and gazebos are good places for hanging baskets, if you are willing to water them consistently.** Add summer color to the shade beneath trees, arbors, and gazebos by hanging baskets of trailing fuchsias, tuberous begonias, or New Guinea impatiens. Warm breezes dry out hanging containers even more quickly than pots at ground level, so you may need to water twice a day.

147 **Add a few late surprises to your pots.** Most of the Pacific Northwest has a long growing season extending well into the fall. It's wise to tuck some chrysanthemums, dahlias, or castor bean (*Ricinus*) into your containers for late summer and fall. Freshen up pots by replacing those annuals that look a bit frayed in August. Pull out leggy petunias and spent nasturtiums and substitute trailing verbena or signet marigolds (*Tagetes tenuifolia*). Fall-flowering sedums such as 'Vera Jameson', 'Ruby Glow', or *Sedum sieboldii* can be used at the rim of the pot for late color, or grown in individual pots as late features.

148 **Use structural plants in containers for focal points.** Plants with bold linear leaves, such as New Zealand flax (*Phormium tenax*) and *Cordyline australis*, create a sense of drama. Use these architectural plants to mark the entry to a new garden space, or to draw attention to the end of a vista.

149 **Take advantage of annuals with colored leaves to enrich your color schemes.** Bronze New Zealand flax (*Phormium tenax* 'Atropurpureum') and bronze cordyline (*Cordyline australis* 'Atropurpurea') have chocolate-colored leaves which combine well with trailing gray-leaved *Helichrysum petiolarum* or gray-green *Helichrysum* 'Limelight'. *Phormium tenax* 'Maori Maiden', 'Maori Chief', 'Maori Sunrise', and 'Flamingo' have rich pink tones in their leaves–plant these with *Diascia* *rigescens,* a draper with dark green leaves and pink flowers, for a color echo.

ESPECIALLY FRAGRANT FLOWERS

150 **Winter daphne (*Daphne odora*) has such delicious perfume that it should be placed near the front door or wherever you are likely to pass by in February.** I see evergreen winter daphne in old established gardens, so I know it can survive the coldest of our winters in the Pacific Northwest if it is planted in a sheltered spot, protected from winter winds. A courtyard is perfect. Daphnes are fussy about good drainage and difficult to transplant. To amend heavy clay soil so that it drains better, add plenty of sand, pumice, and compost to the original dirt. Winter daphne grows 3 to 4 feet tall and spreads even wider as it matures.

151 **For an easier daphne, grow the deciduous *Daphne burkwoodii* 'Somerset'.** A 4- to 5-foot upright plant, 'Somerset' daphne is totally covered with small pink flowers in April. It has a lovely scent that drifts through the spring garden. Small gray-green leaves add to the plant's attractive appearance after bloom time.

152 **It wouldn't be spring in the Pacific Northwest without the opulent flowers and soft sweet fragrance of lilacs.** Ideal for an informal hedge or backdrop for perennial borders, lilacs offer showy flowers in shades of lavender, reddish-purple, and white. If you don't have room for the standard forms, which will grow 12 feet tall in time, plant a dwarf such as Meyer's lilac (*Syringa meyeri*) with smaller, fragrant flowers. Lilacs appreciate lime, especially if your soil is acidic.

153 **Search out and plant the plum tart iris (*Iris gramineus*) for delightful scent and delicate beauty.** "Isn't that a little doll?" a veteran gardener asked me, as she held out a flower for me to sniff. It was the plum tart iris, an unusual perennial that smells like ripe plums and blooms in late spring. Graceful violet flowers with tiny stripes at the tips of the petals nestle in grassy foliage. This 1-foot-tall iris makes a lovely accent at the front of a border that gets at least 6 hours of sun.

◆154◆ **For a piercing sweet fragrance that drifts through the entire garden, plant a mock orange or two.** In late spring, just about the same time as the old roses bloom, mock orange (*Philadelphus*) opens its white flowers. One branch, cut for a bouquet, is enough to scent a room. There are many species and hybrids to choose from. In my own garden, an old, leggy shrub that I inherited from the prior owner fits the description for *Philadelphus* 'Virginal': "the most popular, but it makes a rather awkward bush to display its cupped double, fragrant flowers, borne in profusion." (Graham Stuart Thomas, *Ornamental Shrubs, Climbers and Bamboos*.) Its white flowers enhance the pink and velvety-red old roses that bloom nearby. I am also partial to 'Belle Etoile', a more compact mock orange that has large single flowers with distinctive mauve centers.

◆155◆ **Enjoy lemon lily (*Hemerocallis flava*)–it's the earliest daylily to bloom, opening its piercingly fragrant yellow flowers in May.** Each spring I am pleasantly surprised by the strong sweet smell of lemon lily when its yellow trumpets accompany blue *Geranium pratense* and pink peonies in my front border. Daylilies are great plants in the Pacific Northwest, putting up with standing water in winter and drought in summer.

156 **If you like the scent of vanilla, you will love valerian (*Valeriana officinalis*).** Spikes of lacy-looking white flowers bloom along 4-foot stems in late spring, sending vanilla perfume through the garden. Valerian runs rapidly underground, so you must pull much of it out firmly after it's done flowering to keep it from getting out of hand.

157 **For a cottage garden mood and the sweet and spicy fragrance of cloves, be sure to include an assortment of pinks (*Dianthus*) in sunny places.** Cottage pinks (*Dianthus plumarius*) and their hybrids, sweet William (*Dianthus barbatus*) and *Dianthus superbus* are just a few of my favorite scented pinks. *Dianthus* 'Inchmery', with double, pale pink flowers, is lovely draping over a wall or a sidewalk. Sweet William offers an incredible range of colors—white, pink, fuschia—even black-red. *Dianthus superbus* is the most intoxicatingly fragrant pink, with dainty, fringed flowers—it blooms on long stems, perfect for bouquets. All *Dianthus* are easily propagated by seed and by cuttings.

◆158◆ In shady borders, plant sweet cicely (*Myrrhis odorata*) for fragrance and delicate texture. Sweet cicely blooms in late spring, with lacy white flowers at the tops of ferny leaves. Its seeds have an anise flavor—they may be added to salads. Sweet cicely self-sows but surplus seedlings are easy to pull out.

◆159◆ Masterwort (*Astrantia major*) is invaluable in the shade for fragrant flowers that bloom all summer long. Masterwort has handsome lobed leaves and cream-colored flowers with sweet perfume. It contrasts well with bold hostas and ferny astilbes. Cultivars such as 'Rosea' and 'Prima Donna' have pink flowers. Masterwort does well in shade or morning sun and appreciates generous watering.

◆160◆ *Hosta plantaginea* has the best fragrance of all the plantain lilies. Lettuce-green leaves that have less slug appeal than many other hostas, and deliciously sweet-smelling white flowers in August, make *Hosta* *plantaginea* popular. I grow it at the edge of an island bed for easy sniffing, with pinkish-lavender *Astilbe tacquetii* 'Superba' behind it.

161 **Chocolate cosmos (*Cosmos atrosanguineus*) is a guilt-free garden thrill, its dark red flowers emanating the aroma of chocolate.** This gorgeous foot-tall annual has flowers like a cosmos and leaves like a dahlia. I like it best in pots where its wine-colored blooms are closer to eye and nose level. Try it with blue-violet Swan River daisies and pink or white African daisies (*Osteospermum*).

162 **Annual heliotrope (*Heliotropium arborescens*) combines the richness of purple and the delightful scent of vanilla.** A bit fussy in the ground, heliotrope performs like a trooper in containers–its big heads of purple flowers and dark leaves add an exotic touch. Heliotrope is a thirsty plant, so give it plenty of water.

163 **Countless fragrant lilies are yours to choose from and enjoy if you give the bulbs good drainage.** In the Pacific Northwest, heavy soil and abundant rainfall can spell rot for lilies, but raised beds prevent the problem.

My favorites are regal lily (*Lilium regale*) with maroon buds that open to white trumpets, 'Pink Perfection', 'Golden Splendor', and pure white 'Casa Blanca'.

164 Enjoy the sweet smell of honeysuckle in winter and summer by choosing two varieties. Rare, but worth searching for, *Lonicera standishii* is a shrubby honeysuckle that can be trained to climb a low fence or railing. Creamy-white, scented flowers appear surprisingly in winter. Common as cucumbers, summer-blooming Hall's honeysuckle (*Lonicera japonica halliana*) is so piercingly fragrant that I must have two—one covers a stump in the front garden, a second climbs a large arch in the backyard. This second honeysuckle is extremely vigorous, good for hiding eyesores, and very easy to propagate from tip cuttings.

165 Take advantage of roses, for they offer more summer color and fragrance than any flower genus. The difficulty is narrowing down the abundant choices. My friend Ruth Mackey, a fragrance connoisseur, recommends 'Prospero', a velvety red English rose. She says it smells like rose petals with sugar added. To my less discerning nose, rugosa roses smell heavenly, especially 'Hansa', with bright deep pink flowers and whopper hips. A whiff of the double pink damask rose, 'La Vie de Bruxelles', or the purple-red moss 'William Lobb', is intoxicating.

166 **Enjoy evening perfume in the garden by growing flowering tobacco (*Nicotiana*).** My garden is scented every summer night by pure white nicotiana 'Jasmine', a 3-foot-tall beauty, and *Nicotiana sylvestris*, with large, tropical-looking leaves and white tubular flowers.

167 **Grow scented geraniums for the pungent perfume of their leaves.** I love to mix rose-scented geranium (*Pelargonium graveolens*) into containers so that I can rub the leaves when I'm watering and release the heavenly fragrance. Peppermint-scented geranium (*Pelargonium tomentosum*) is not only refreshing but also velvety.

168 **For a fragrant path, plant lemon thyme (*Thymus citriodorus*) and Corsican mint (*Mentha requienii*) between paving stones.** Lemon thyme and Corsican mint both release their refreshing aromas when brushed against, or crushed underfoot.

Lemon thyme prefers sun and good drainage, while the tiny-leaved Corsican mint will grow anywhere, often seeding itself where you least expect it.

169 **Pots of lemon-scented verbena (*Aloysia triphylla*) and pineapple sage (*Salvia rutilans*) have strong fruity scents and tolerate summer's heat.** Although these herbs are annual and must be replaced each year, I love to grow them for their enjoyable fragrance. They make charming garnishes for iced tea and fruit salads.

SOURCES FOR PLANTS AND SEEDS

170 The most economical way to start plants is from seed, but you must exercise patience. For a dollar or two, a packet of viable seed will be worth its weight in gold. The expenditure will be the time it will take you to order and germinate the seeds, nurture and protect the seedlings, and wait for the plants to bloom. In the case of perennials and bulbs it may take two years before you see flowers.

171 Although it's convenient to have a greenhouse, it's easy to start seeds indoors if you provide warmth, consistent moisture, and

sterile soil. I start my seeds in trays saved from annuals. I fill them with sterile potting soil, sprinkle seed on the surface, cover lightly with a little more potting soil. I place the trays inside plastic sweater boxes, and water thoroughly from below by pouring about an inch of water into the boxes—this avoids washing away the seeds. I use room temperature water mixed with a quarter-strength solution of fungicide to prevent damping off, a fungus disease that makes new seedlings wilt and die. Then I cover the boxes and place them in a warm dark place until the seedlings pop up.

⟨172⟩ **Once seedlings germinate, grow them in a greenhouse, on a sunny windowsill, or under fluorescent lights.** I take the lids off the sweater boxes and place them underneath 4-foot fluorescent lights, with one warm and one cool light in each fixture. The lights hang from chains attached to hooks in the ceiling. By using S-hooks between the fixtures and the chains I can raise the fixtures by shortening the chains as the plants grow taller. I keep the seedlings a constant 6 inches from the lightbulbs, so that they grow steadily and compactly. I water from below with a quarter-strength solution of 20-20-20 fertilizer, and keep the lights on timers for 16 hours daily.

173 For best results, start your seedlings about eight weeks before you plan to plant them outdoors. It takes most seedlings a few days to a week or two to sprout (there are exceptions that take as long as two years, and a good reference book will inform you) and another six weeks or so to get big enough to face the great outdoors.

174 Be sure to harden off seedlings for a few days before planting, and protect their tender young leaves from hungry slugs. It's a big shock for plants that have been coddled in a warm indoor environment to suddenly encounter bright sunlight and pelting rains. To help them make the transition gradually, harden them off by setting them in a shady, sheltered place for a couple of days before planting. Protect them from slugs by using your favorite bait (see tip 195). If possible, keep flats of seedlings up on a table high enough off the ground to minimize the danger of being gobbled up by slugs.

175 Experiment by starting plants from cuttings outdoors—you will be pleasantly surprised at how easy this can be. I've had excellent results starting the following plants from tip cuttings in springtime: sedums, chrysanthemums, butterfly bush (*Buddleia*), tree mallow (*Lavatera*), rugosa roses, and penstemon hybrids. Choose stems that are young and firm, before the plant sets buds, and snip off 6-inch tip cuttings. Remove the lower leaves and cut the upper leaves in half, then stick the cuttings into flats filled with damp sand. Make inch-deep holes, place each cutting in a hole, tamp the sand firmly around each cutting to prevent air pockets, and gently water the flats with a wand. Test the cuttings after a couple of months by tugging on them. Resistance means they've formed roots, and it's time to pot them up.

176 **The easiest way to propagate perennials is from divisions.** Most perennials can be increased by lifting the plant and separating it into sections. The best time to do this is before or after flowering. Water the plant well first, to ease digging it up, place it on a tarp for convenience, and separate it into several pieces, each with stems and roots attached. If the root system is very dense—this is common with daylilies, Siberian iris, and ornamental grasses—you may need to chop the plant apart with an ax. Sometimes it helps to soak tough customers in a bucket overnight to loosen the soil around the roots.

177 **Perennials that spread by rhizomes are also very easy to propagate.** Many of the hardy cranesbills, especially *Geranium ibericum*, *Geranium endressii*, and *Geranium cantabrigiense*, run along on woody surface roots. In mid-spring when the plants are vigorously spreading, it's a snap to pull a side shoot off with its rhizomes attached. Stick each chunk into a pot filled with good soil, and cut back most of the top foliage. Water well, and wait a few weeks. New leaves will grow while new roots fill the pot.

178 **For the best information and healthiest plants, find a nursery run by professional growers.** A nursery staffed with professionals may charge a little more for plants than a discount supermarket but will save you money in the long run with good advice and well-grown plants. Your best bet is a nursery that grows and sells its own stock from scratch—they will know the conditions the plants need to thrive. Next best is a garden center that buys material from the growers and distributes it to the public, with experienced staff to take good care of the plants and answer your questions knowledgeably.

179 A healthy plant looks vigorous, with roots that fill the pot and no insects, black spot, or mildew on the leaves. To choose the best plant, look for one that is well-branched and not yet flowering—it will grow more side stems and produce a bigger specimen once you get it in the ground. A taller plant on a single stem is less desirable, for it will become leggy.

180 If a plant looks suspiciously small in a big container, give a gentle pull on the stem. If it feels loose, don't buy it. Many plants are grown from liners, small plants that are essentially rooted cuttings, potted into gallons until they mature. If they're sold too soon you may be paying a gallon's price for a cutting's worth of plant.

181 Mail-order nurseries are great opportunities to find what is not available locally. First shop locally for your plants, so you can see the plant in person and pick the best of the batch. But when the plants aren't on hand, look for them in catalogues. Try mail-order sources closer to home first. Shipping time is shorter and easier on the plants, and growing conditions are most like your own.

182 Before you order from a catalogue, ask how the plants are shipped, and what size plant you can expect to receive. Plant sizes and packaging methods vary a lot from nursery to nursery. Some states are required to ship bare-root plants to the Pacific Northwest because of our agricultural regulations–this is hard on the plants. A plant protected by soil around its roots and wrapped in damp paper will make an easier transition. Some nurseries ship the equivalent of a 4-inch pot, others send a rooted cutting–find out first which you can expect to avoid disappointment.

183 When it comes to bulbs, check the shipping and handling charges. They can make the cost of the bulbs prohibitive. A few bulb vendors send their bulbs freight-free, and those are the ones to select from first. Then, you may want to order bulbs by mail that you can't find anywhere locally and accept the extra shipping charges as a necessary evil.

184 Buying bulbs in large numbers can save you a lot of money. Most bulb nurseries discount larger quantities of bulbs. Mixed colors are also often less expensive. Consider splitting an order with several gardening friends to take advantage of bulk prices. Some catalogues offer discounts for early orders and bonus bulbs for orders over a certain price.

◆185◆ Remember to order peonies, Japanese iris, Siberian iris, and Spuria iris in the spring or summer for fall shipment. Gardeners must plan ahead, especially when it comes to ordering plants that are shipped when they're dormant. It's frustrating to see beautiful peonies and beardless iris blooming in early summer and not be able to buy plants right then. Patience and perseverance! Visit your local specialty growers during bloom time and place your order for fall shipping, or send for catalogues and order by mail.

◆186◆ Reputable nurseries will offer a replacement plant if you report any problems with shipping immediately. Most mail-order firms understand that some plants may suffer in transit and they will make good the loss if you notify them promptly. However, they can't be expected to replace plants that don't thrive after you've planted them, for too many variables (insects, predators, weather, poor soil) can affect a plant's survival.

187 Many horticultural and plant societies have seed exchanges and plant sales that are great for finding the new and unusual. Societies exist for just about every kind of plant you want to study. Some, such as The American Penstemon Society, are organized by genus, while others, such as The American Rock Garden Society, study larger groups of plants by culture. For a complete listing, see the latest edition of *Gardening by Mail* by Barbara J. Barton.

188 For access to unusual plants, join overseas plant societies with seed-exchange benefits. The Scottish Rock Garden Club, The Hardy Plant Society of Great Britain, The Society for Growing Australian Plants, The New Zealand Alpine Garden Society, The Alpine Garden Club of British Columbia, and The Alpine Garden Society (Great Britain) allow members to order seed for very reasonable prices. See the Horticultural Societies section of *Gardening by Mail* for detailed current information.

189 If you're hunting for new and unusual plants, it's easy to order seeds from overseas catalogues. Those who like to find something different for their gardens will be excited by the Chiltern Seeds catalogue (Chiltern Seeds, Bortree Stile, Ulverston, Cumbria LA12 7PB, England, send four dollar bills). The first time I saw it was in a friend's bathroom, and she wondered if I was taking a bath.

190 **Check with your county extension service for information about plant sales and educational opportunities.** Many counties have Master Gardener programs designed to teach you all about gardening. Classes are free—you pay by volunteering your time to educate the public. Master Gardener chapters often hold plant sales and host educational booths at county fairs, horticultural shows, and nurseries.

191 **The best way to save money on plants is to swap divisions, cuttings, and seeds with your friends.** Gardeners are a generous group—often all you have to do is admire a plant and they will offer to save you seed or hand you a cutting. Sharing plants can be the beginning of new friendships that go on and on just like the perennials do.

192 **Offer to help a gardening friend weed, and inevitably you will go home with some plants.** Siberian and bearded iris, lamb's ears, feverfew, love-in-a-mist, and loosestrife are just a few of many plants that multiply beyond the needs of any garden, and must be thinned or weeded out. An experienced gardener's weeds can become your new plants if you're there at the right time—otherwise they'll end up on the compost pile.

KEEPING YOUR GARDEN HEALTHY

❀ ❀ ❀

193 **In my garden an insect is a pest if it's destroying the plants.** I don't mind if a bug wants a bite or two of a hosta's leaf, as long as they're not eating the whole thing for dinner. When a plant is severely weakened and can't bloom I take action.

194 **Some insects cause a little damage that is mostly cosmetic–leave them alone and spare yourself the danger and expense of toxic sprays.** Spit bugs are a good example of nuisances that are pretty innocuous. The foamy white blobs of "spit" in which they live are unattractive, but they don't do any damage to the lavender hedge where they like to hang out in my garden. Sometimes I hose them off, or remove them by hand, but mostly I tell myself, "Oh, the spit bugs are here, it must be June."

195 **In the wet areas of the Pacific Northwest, slugs do the most damage to plants, and preventive measures should be taken year-round.** Fall cleanup of leaf litter and weeds will help to prevent slugs from hiding out in their favorite environment—damp, decaying debris. Some gardeners swear by copper barrier wire, diatomaceous earth, and pumice to keep slugs out of beds and borders. Many successfully bait with saucers of beer—the slugs drink the stuff, fall in, and drown. Metaldehyde-based poisons should be used cautiously because your pets may decide to take a taste. The pellet forms have been known to sicken dogs and cats, and even the liquid form can be dangerous to cats that dig around it and lick their paws.

196 **The least toxic way to get rid of pests is removing them by hand.** The more I learn how many pesticides make us sick, the more willing I am to hand-pick the bad bugs. I wear surgical gloves, then collect slugs in a coffee can and put the lid on. You can also put down boards or upside-down grapefruit halves. At night the slugs will hide underneath these damp places, and in the morning you will have easy pickings. I hose aphids off the rose buds with a strong spray of water, or remove them by hand. Often if I wait a day or two the ladybugs will have arrived to the rescue.

197 **Attracting birds to your garden will cut down on the aphid population.** Bird feeders, a water source, and fruiting trees and shrubs will encourage insect-eating birds to naturally cut down on your pests. Ducks are champion slug hunters.

198 **Learn to tell the difference between the good guys and the bad guys by consulting bug books.** The *Audubon Field Guide to North American Butterflies* has photographs of the eggs and caterpillars of butterflies so that you don't kill a Monarch butterfly larva, mistaking it for a European Cabbage White caterpillar about to gobble up your nasturtiums.

199 Steer clear of plants susceptible to diseases and substitute hardier look-alikes. The third year my lupines were covered with aphids I gave up and replaced them with speedwells (*Veronica spicata*) and foxgloves (*Digitalis purpurea*) that gave me columnar flowers without grief. When I was convinced that hollyhocks always got rust no matter where I planted them, I pulled them out and planted marsh mallows (*Hibiscus moscheutos*), hollyhock mallows (*Malva alcea*), and tree mallows (*Lavatera thuringiaca*).

200 In the wetter zones of the Pacific Northwest you will have healthier plants if you grow hybrid musks and rugosa roses instead of Bourbons. Although Bourbon roses have fragrant, cup-shaped flowers, their leaves are very prone to black spot and mildew. Hybrid musk and rugosa roses are just as beautiful and also resistant to these fungal diseases.

SUGGESTED READING

Barbara J. Barton. *Gardening by Mail, A Source Book*. Boston: Houghton Mifflin Company, 1990.

Clausen, Ruth Rogers and Ekstrom, Nicolas H. *Perennials for American Gardens*. New York: Random House, 1989.

Harper, Pamela J. *Color Echoes, Harmonizing Color in the Garden*. New York: Macmillan Publishing Company, 1994.

Proctor, Rob. *Annuals*, New York: Running Heads Incorporated, 1991.

Pyle, Robert Michael. *The Audubon Society Field Guide to North American Butterflies*. New York: Alfred A. Knopf, 1981.

Starcher, Allison Mia. *Good Bugs for Your Garden*. Chapel Hill, North Carolina: Algonquin Books of Chapel Hill, 1995.

The Editors of Sunset Books and Sunset Magazine. *The Western Garden Annual*. Menlo Park, California: Lane Publishing Company, 1995.

The Staff of "Organic Gardening" Magazine. *The Encyclopedia of Organic Gardening*. Emmaus, Pennsylvania: Rodale Press, 1985.

Thomas, Graham Stuart. *Ornamental Shrubs, Climbers and Bamboos*. Portland, Oregon: Timber Press Inc., 1992.

Thomas, Graham Stuart. *Shrub Roses of Today*. London: J. M. Dent & Sons Ltd., 1985.

INDEX

Please note: the numbers below refer to the tips, not the book's pages.